NAMING
RITES

BOOKS BY GARY BOELHOWER

Naming Rites—Poems,
Holy Cow! Press (2017)

Choose Wisely: Practical Insights from Spiritual Traditions,
Paulist Press (2013)

Mountain 10: Climbing the Labyrinth Within,
(co-authored with Joe Miguez and Tricia Pearce)
Mountain Ten Resources (2013)

Marrow, Muscle, Flight—Poems,
Wildwood River Press (2011)

NAMING
RITES

Poems by Gary Boelhower

Holy Cow! Press

Duluth, Minnesota

2017

Cover painting, "Ediacara," by Kate Whittaker.

Author photograph by Amanda Hansmeyer.

Book and cover design by Anton Khodakovsky.

Printed and bound in the United States of America.

First printing, Spring, 2017

ISBN 978-0-9864480-7-2

10 9 8 7 6 5 4 3 2 1

Acknowledgements: Thank you to the editors of the following journals and anthologies where the following poems first appeared, sometimes in earlier versions:

America: Jacob's Ladder

Amethyst and Agate: Poems of Lake Superior: Dance at Dawn

The Freshwater Review: Like a Mystic, Dance at Dawn, Chopping Birch, Colombia Displaced

Labyrinth Pathways: Give Yourself

New Millenium Writings: Human Robotics Project

Prove: Language Acquisition

Shavings: Ancient Grains

Holy Cow! Press projects are funded in part by grant awards from the Ben and Jeanne Overman Charitable Trust, the Elmer L. and Eleanor J. Andersen Foundation, the Cy and Paula DeCosse Fund of The Minneapolis Foundation, the Lenfestey Family Foundation, and by gifts from generous individual donors.

Holy Cow! Press books are distributed to the trade by Consortium Book Sales & Distribution, c/o Ingram Publisher Services, Inc., 210 American Drive, Jackson, TN 38301.

For inquiries, please write to:

Holy Cow! Press, Post Office Box 3170, Mount Royal Station, Duluth, MN 55803.

Visit www.holycowpress.org

For my mother *Minnie Boelhower* who showed me how to pay attention to the world's beauty and its songs. For poets *Pamela Mittlefehldt* and *Sheila Packa* who provide constant inspiration and insightful critique. For poet *Deborah Cooper* and the participants in our classes at the Saint Louis County jail who prove again and again that the light searches out every aperture. For *Jim Perlman* for believing in this collection of poems. For my sister *Susan Griffiths* and my brother *William Boelhower* who have blessed me with family who explore ideas and love poetry and story. For my spouse *Gary Braden Anderson* whose tender touch shapes the clay of me precious day by precious day.

Contents

I.

II.

III.

IV.

V.

I.

Beginning to Know My Name

I am just beginning to know my name,
to sit in a pool of light without worrying about
tomorrow or how the end will come,
to walk slowly through a green forest without

caring how far I get on the trail. Most of my mail
I do not open, most of the catalogs I do not read.
I prefer children on the beach with shovel and pail.
I have begun to know the difference between want and need.

Still, I catch myself wanting to name the mystery.
Then, I remember I belong to the silence, and my sacred tryst
is with sunlight on the Baptism river. I kneel in the birch wood
listening to the water surrender. My work is gratitude.

Hide and Seek

I hide under grandpa's porch in the scary dark,
shoulder to cold cinder block, spider webs and smell
of rot, hoping to be found, to be touched. I stay there
a long time until I realize they don't care about finding me.

I am hidden inside the skin that will not fit,
the rules and regulations, the holy definitions
of sin and grace. I know it first as difference,
not being happy with baseball or wrestling.

I take a blanket and an orange to my refuge
in the woods, content to watch the green ferns
unfurl and listen to the blue river sing
its constant song of mercy and desire.

Wanting to be found, to be seen, I memorize
all the answers in the catechism and win
the glow-in-the-dark statue of Mary in second grade,
and even the eighth-graders listen when I recite poetry.

When I fill out the application to the seminary,
there is the question about being feminine—code
words I do not know; the name for it no one speaks.
I am left to wonder about my difference and my dreams.

Then his lips send the soft shiver of certain knowledge
coursing from cell to cell, filling the spaces between
the electrons, spiraling to the center of my mystery.
I am found, touched in the dark. I know the name

of my need, the covenant written in my blood.
But every love must be hidden, no songs can be
sung to the bright sky, to the dancing flowers.
They all go their way carrying their dark secrets.

There is only one answer played out on the movie screens,
written in the rule books, chanted in the church.
Happiness is marriage and children, work that
matters, a name spoken with recognition and respect.

I shut the box tight, nail the lid fast with promises,
step into the self that hopes and prays itself to exist.
Love answers to the cries of children in the dark,
fills the hollows of the bones with stories of baseball games,

dance recitals, debates, soccer matches, and the marching band.
I find a life overflowing with three precious promises,
balancing their bicycles until they pedal off into confidence,
the gift of hearing them shout their own names into the sky.

Faithful to my unfaithfulness, perhaps there was something
in me she knew she could not satisfy. The divorce
almost drowns me, months in tears and tectonic questions,
until I see the chance to seek a life that bears my whole name,

to join love and longing, to shed the darkness of the hiding place,
to be found, touched, to say my name and his name together in the light.

Word

I spent most of my growing summers on my uncle's green farm.
He worked nights in the factory, days in the fields, and knew
the ache and joy of a dream. So every hand was welcome
and something cellular in me longed for the farm's rituals,
its stretching horizon, its lessons simple as seed.

Cutting alfalfa in the shiver of an early morning, oily warmth
coming off the tractor's engine, sweet perfume rising
from the severed stalks, then, a feast of breakfast and milk
full of cream from last night's milking. All gathered in the warm
kitchen, everyone's role in the day ahead laid out like dance steps.

I remember the day I promised to fill the water tank
before the lumbering cows, each with a name, came
home from pasture. Cows don't give milk unless
they drink water. And I forgot. My uncle took me aside:
"Your word must mean something." No lecture, no
long examples. That evening, he told me to carry carefully
the pails after each cow was milked, pail after pail half empty.

And still I name my deepest longing a word that means
something, a word made flesh, no difference between
the promise and the act. Word, true as milk and bread,
light the stars again and let me not forget to be what I have spoken.

Preparing the Soil

I don't know how old I was
but I can hear the labor of the old Farmall
pulling the drag over the clumps and clods
of red clay, taste the oily heat
coming off the engine as I sit beside
my favorite uncle, see the long wide acres stretching
under a rolling, roiling sky.
I wasn't old enough to drive but I could watch
for rocks where we would make our next pass
over the land, big rocks that would break
the teeth or bend a bar,
rocks that kept rising up out of the earth
year after year.
Above us the clouds were moving
on this spring day,
arranging and rearranging themselves
into mounds and mountains with the blue thunder
gathering in their bellies,
the thunder we were racing against
to get the seed planted before the rain.
When we had passed over the field twice,
first running north to south,
then east to west, we stopped on the edge
of the field and my uncle
got down off the tractor and I followed
without knowing why. I thought
we would be rushing to get the grain drill
and start the planting.

He settled into a knee bend
and took a scoop of soil with both hands,
bringing his hands together under the dirt
to lift the soil like an offering
or a prayer.
I crouched beside him and he told me
to feel the soil. He said
It's ready now, fine, warm, ready.
And then he opened his fingers just a little
and let the dirt sift slowly through them.
And there on the edge of the field
with the dirt in my hands
it all connected,
the ashes
from Ash Wednesday a few weeks before
pressed onto my forehead,
the drone of the priest, thou art dust,
the grit falling
onto my eyelashes and my nose,
what gives us life
and takes our life at the end.
The whole immense rhythm
rising out of the earth, I knew
everything was moving, even the earth
was shifting, rising, breathing, everything
was moving in waves, music, birth, some immense
rhythm moving in the guts
of all things.

Grandma's Names

Her name sounds like feathers,
matches the slight build of her body,
the sweet thin crust of her gooseberry pie,
the dance of her fingers twisting filaments to lace.

When the moon hangs like a hammered shield
she tells us the names of grandfathers and grandmothers
and the names of the ships of their journey,
the names of their children
petting the dogs each with a name
who herded the cows each with a name,
nipping at their hooves all the way home.

She passes the name of the cool spring
from lip to lip with each pure cup,
the name of the creek's bend where the watercress
sighs in the lengthening light,
the name of the old road where the asparagus triumphs
in the ditches on mornings dew wet and wild with grace.

She knows the names of the stars,
traces the stories of light with her hooked finger
on the map of velvet summer nights,
sings the songs of bear and swan,
king and archer with arrows of fire.

She whispers the names under our skin,
sings them into our tender yearning bones
until we feel at home walking in the genesis garden
and safe under the dancing midnight sky.

Sitting in Sunlight

She is sitting in a small patch of sunlight that streams
in the window in a quiet corner away from the TV
and the craft table, close to the artificial tree

with its canned pine scent that lingers in the social
room and mixes with the faint odors of age.
Her face, the color of yellowed parchment.

Paper thin skin stretched taught, the pulse
of blood just under the surface of the back of her hands.
When I ask about Christmas as a child,

she begins remembering, like peeling an orange
in one continuous strand, the released
fragrance of childhood fills her face.

It is as if the question gives her permission to open
a door that has been locked. She directs me
with her tiny voice to walk down the stairs of memory,

to light a candle in the hidden treasure house of her life.
She talks of ribbon candy, undulating flow
of confection sometimes three inches long, playful

colors, the taste of it even before it touches your tongue
and then the full flavor. Memories visit in the warming
patch of sunlight in the slow afternoon of winter.

She talks of those moments just after holiday dawn,

of her small hand searching in the stocking,
thrusting past the nuts and the orange lodged in the heel,

down to the toe where the pieces of sheer delight are waiting,
for sure, you can count on it like your mother's love.
"What's the best gift you ever got?" I ask.

"It was the same every year," she says. "Mother coaxed
us out of sleep when it was still dark, bundled us warm
with coats, boots, mittens. We stepped into the brittle cold.

Hand in hand we walked toward the east singing
Christmas songs. Soon the dawn would break above the trees
and paint the clouds pink and purple like ribbon candy

streaming across the sky. We walked into the light,
felt it on our faces. Then we tried to run in our clumsy boots
back home to find a little tree in the corner of the kitchen

hung with tinsel, stockings full, father smiling."
"And the best gift," I ask again. "It was the light,
the tender light." White flakes of silence drift around us,

sift between our sentences as afternoon shadows lengthen.
Her eyes full of memories. I lean into the light and hold her hand.

Second Grade Lessons

They closed Holy Name of Jesus school for a week
after the explosion when I was in second grade.
My uncle John and the old Dutch pastor
were killed on a cold Saturday morning
by the blast from the boiler, the wall and blackboard
in my classroom were cracked and the windows
shattered. Someone said the outline of the priest's body
was imprinted on the wall of the boiler room but
I didn't see it because second graders were not allowed
to go down there. They replaced the windows, hung
a shiny green board, and repaired the wall but I could
still see the cracks under the fresh paint. That first day back
when everyone was working very hard as we were told
I could hear Dennis Vanderveldon breathing behind me
scratching his number two pencil to fill in the blanks
under the pictures and I could feel the boiler below us,
the slight shifts and rumbles through the floor. They
told us everything would be OK. I stared and stared
at the letters, capital and lower case, marching across the top
of the new green board and the whole classroom
filled with failure from the aluminum chalk tray
with its long white pieces of silent chalk to the waxed
wooden floor that smelled a little like danger.
The room got smaller and smaller and not even Sister
Michael's big rosary hanging at her waist could save us.

In Grandpa's Back Yard

Everything about him was mysterious to my child eyes.
He shaved with a straight razor. Slapped the cutting edge
back and forth in perfect rhythm against the leather strap
to hone the blade, held that sharp steel to his neck every
morning. His body was fashioned from hardwood,
straight, strong, unyielding, not a bit of dance or flow.
He seldom smiled. One finger cut off above the knuckle.
A hearing aid that buzzed so loud he just blankly
nodded when you asked him a question.

He loved to work even at eighty and ninety.
Tended his acre of garden, straight long rows,
every variety of vegetable evenly spaced and tasting
like Eden. On winter days that forced him inside
he would crack hickory nuts with dogged persistence
motivated by some non-negotiable quota
divinely revealed to him alone. Daily he would take
his three Dutch prayer books and walk to church
to spend a few hours with the Lord. I don't know
if he was doing time for past sins or continuing
his arguments before the ultimate tribunal.
Frayed collars and cuffs, patched black jacket,
one pocket ripped off. He never wore anything new,
luxury and excess were not allowed. Every night
before he went to bed he drank one shot
of blackberry brandy from the bottle he kept
in his dresser, one shot, no more no less.

And so I could hardly believe it when he called us all
to his backyard one bright summer afternoon.
He had placed two flower stands twenty feet apart.
On one, balanced on a pivot, an old tarnished silver spoon
holding half a potato. On the other a wine glass glinting
in sunlight. With one quick flick of his finger
he sent the potato flying through space, tumbling perfectly
toward the other stand twenty feet away. The half of potato,
round end down, dropped exactly in the waiting wine glass.

He cackled, not a mild laugh, but glee bubbled out
of him. Only once, no repeat performance. Then back
to work, shovel on his shoulder to the garden,
leaving us standing in the green grass with our questions.
It was the first and last time I heard my grandpa giggle
but after that everything was possible.

Mother's Story

Every few years she would mention it,
usually after church on the first Friday.
I would ask her to tell me again.
She would make tea
and we would sit in the kitchen sunlight.

In Detroit, young mother, trying to make ends meet,
she works for the couple in the upstairs apartment.
Washes clothes with bleach, irons shirts with starch,
does dishes with detergent, cleans floors
meticulous with ammonia, soap and water all day long.
Her hands turn red, then deep sores that won't go away.
The doctor prescribes creams and ointments,
some of them bluish white and thin like mother's milk,
some thick, oozing gray that smell like the cheese
my father loves, and all of them sting.
She winces with every application before she slides
her hands into the long rubber gloves
that might protect her from further harm.
Month after month the doctor offers
another remedy. Nothing works. Her raw
flesh weeps its own kind of tears.

Then she hears of Casey at the Friary,
brown-robed Brother with a long white beard.
That Sunday she takes the bus, stands in the hopeful line
for three hours outside the weathered wooden doors
that look like they are made from Jesus' cross.
She kneels before him. He takes her hands in his.

"My hands just don't get better,
none of the prescriptions help. I have to work."
His thin lips whisper a prayer.
She feels it in her body. "Your hands will be better
by Friday. Perhaps, you could attend Mass
on the first Fridays for the next year to say thank you."
He blesses her and she sees a tender light in his wrinkled face.

She never missed first Friday Mass. She heard
that whispered prayer, saw that tender light every month
as she would fold her thankful hands.

Apple Pilgrimage

A chorus line of geese honking hosannas
pulls us toward the orchard,
annual pilgrimage in orange October.

The breeze clatters through the cornstalks
and coaxes leaves into wild kite stunts,
flashing colors rise and dive.

Glow of goldfish fin, dance of flame,
finch feather shine,
the colors swoop and sail

until they are gathered into the lap
of the story-telling mother who knows
the rhythm and rhyme of all time.

In the back room of the orchard store,
far from the bales of straw perfectly arranged
to look haphazard for the customer's critical eye,

the apples tumble down the conveyor belt unsorted,
small, large, misshapen, some with blemishes
from summer hail or scars where birds stole

a sweet morsel against the hungry day.
Some are crushed for cider, others sold for cheap
seconds, and some in fine baskets labeled choice.

We never bought from the orchard store.

Mom and I picked the apples off the ground.
We wore clothes left over from the church rummage sale

and the orchard owner gave us windfalls for free.
Some were nearly perfect and in my memory
all of them were sweet. The ritual was exact. The apple

was rubbed to gleaming green and red, then snap
of teeth entering, earth taste of skin, explosion of juice.
Some apples were nearly lost, violence of storm,

rotting in the moist grass, but we piled them all
in our hungry basket. Later, pleading for pie,
I watched her fingers twisted with rheumatism

cut out the bruised flesh with the skill of a surgeon
just down to the white sweet. Peeling only
the thinnest membrane, not to waste a single slice.

Each apple was gift to her, nested in her lap, then turned
in her hand with such close attention, it must have been prayer.

Last Suppers

I'm not sure which one will be the last,
so each time I try to make it perfect,
travel a hundred miles to cook dinner.
I know the end is coming but not how many more
failures of her frail machinery it will take.

I roast the chicken slowly while we talk
about how she made bread every Saturday morning,
smell of yeast filling the house,
swelling promise of dough.
Always one brown loaf cut warm just out of the oven,
slices smeared with butter,
tastes of sunshine, apple and earth.
I tell her no flavor in the world has ever come close.

I baste the browning breast with juices
every twenty minutes, which gives her a little rest.
Just paying attention is exhausting now.
With each trip into the small kitchen
the swirling currents of the past
pull at my ankles, as if everything said
and not said around this table runs in a river of memory.
I see spilled milk on the table,
bright finger paintings on the refrigerator door,
school books piled high next to the stack of overdue bills,
the sewing machine and precise patterns that always
had to be altered to fit the remnant of material
we could afford. A spot of sunlight on the worn linoleum
becomes the summer afternoon when my wagon
tipped over and she was there to kiss the bleeding ankle
and rock me until I caught my breath.

I prop up her tiny body with three pillows
in a chair at the table. I serve the baked potato
with a perfect dollop of sour cream,
exactly how she taught me. It was her style,
a statement she made after cleaning
other people's floors and toilets all day.
I take a buttery chunk from the drumstick,
the part she likes the best but always
let me choose first, a spoonful of potato
and three glazed carrot coins, and put it all
in the baby food grinder because today
her throat has become a narrow passage.
When I cradle this spoonful of sweet puree
to her mouth she smiles radiant as the trumpet of a lily.

She has four mouthfuls. I do not admonish her
to eat more, this is not about survival.
After each bite she closes her eyes to savor the taste,
all the simple delights of human flesh, a private
thanksgiving that gathers a lifetime of moments.
Then she opens her small hands in her lap,
lifts them ever so slightly, her palms toward the light.

I Didn't Know

I didn't know you were watching
every step, listening to every word.
I didn't know you were memorizing
the moments, keeping each one
like a small picture in the silver locket
next to your heart. I didn't know
you saved all the finger paintings that faded
on the refrigerator in files
labeled by year, grade, class.
I didn't know every report card
would go into a big manila envelope
packed with bright wishes and hopes
with longings for something more
than the small house and the small paycheck,
not for money or being noticed,
but for beauty and songs,
for the stories that could happen on a stage,
for the books that lined library shelves
in universities, for the paintings
on walls of museums, for the way
a life could blossom from a small closed fist
like the fine silk of a peony
laying itself open in the sun.

Last Time

Closing the door for the last time,
all the rooms echoing emptiness,
the linoleum unscuffed and gleaming,
a storm of voices and images
as I stand on the threshold
staring into the silence.
Rich warmth of yeast
in the busy kitchen,
six loaves of bread baked
every Saturday, cut warm, buttered, good.
All of us gathered around the table,
chairs touching the cupboards
and the walls, scratched Melmac dishes
and three patterns of silverware,
small stove in one corner
with pots and pans simmering
on all four burners,
leftover coffee warming in the saucepan,
sewing machine in the other corner
piled high with patterns and bright remnants
and our longing for jackets from Penney's.
Deep musk of the root cellar
with rows of mason jars
boasting tomatoes, beans, beets.
Prying the paraffin
off the top of the currant jelly.
The garden which took up most
of the back yard, rows upon rows
and a border of flowers, summer feast,

flavors of sun and earth.
As I lock the door and walk away
an orphan,
I hear the ball game
playing on the transistor radio
in the back yard
where my father
sits next to the purple lilacs,
beer bottle by his side in the green grass
in the deep cool shade.

Garden Promises

(for Gary Braden Anderson on our wedding day)

I have flown on the back of the midnight crow
through the cold rains and the dry winds.
I have crawled on the earth when I could
no longer stand its tectonic shifts and betrayals.
I have been carried by the river of joy,
stronger than doubt, stronger than death,
to this threshold, this open field of daisies and decision,
this clearing where you stand at the same door.

At your feet now I lay these humble gifts,
a scattering of seeds, some small as eyelashes,
some hard and armored, some ready to burst into green,
and I am asking if we might plant them together,
if we might be faithful to the rhythms
of orbits and eons together,
to the play of honey light that opens all things to song,
to the patient work of rain that softens and feeds the center,
if we might give ourselves to the tempo of mystery,
the pulse that lives in the earth
and breathes among the galaxies,
the cadence that calls us into the streets with voices
of protest and hope,
give ourselves together to the music
of the eternal loom weaving all things together with
compassion and laughter, mercy and forgiveness,
and the fierce devotion and wide freedom of love.

I know something about gardens
and I am ready to learn more.
I know every year has its own seasons, that there is
drought and plenty, growth and decay,
grief and gratitude. I know there is nothing sweeter
than the ripe moment of gift.
I know all things finally surrender to the earth
and the mystery that cannot be said
despite all our philosophies and all the names of God.
So I humbly promise to sow and harvest,
to weed and water, to sing and be silent.
I promise to tend these days of our togetherness
with compassion and laughter, mercy and forgiveness,
and the fierce devotion and wide freedom of love.

Winter Night

making angels
in drifts of crystals
under the moonlight
soft shadows
of the clouds
lay our bodies down
with their wild wings
fly through the cold stars
white syllables
land on eyelash lip tongue
taste the manna
of winter

and after hot chocolate
breathe together
under the comforter
to make the warm
nest of home
where even our thorns
are holy
sweet musk
of the animal body
small silences between
the ribs
and places
where we catch
on fire
angel savage mercy

Blueberry Picking

When the summer rain is soft
and the pine trunks are wet on one side
and still warm on the other
I try to make up the story
of blue in the blueberries
dusk patina
radiance of deep water
purple cone flower and larkspur
each berry a drop
of almost midnight and luminous dawn
stubborn among the charred trees
fire and storm
blow down and dank decay
still their tiny bold sweetness
I pluck and place by the handfuls
in the mouth of my lover
staining his teeth and lips blue
because finally we must say goodbye
to everyone and everything
we love.

Flight

Cool fuselage of your body
and bright wings fashioned to fly
the hard mechanics of your mercy
lift us into the endless silk of sky
take us shuddering into flight
we breathe the high thin air
journey through the speechless night
climb through the clouds of fear
knowing that when we stop
like Icarus we will drop
into the ordinary night
where moths at the lamp
fling themselves toward the light.

Call Me by That Name

Lay another log on the embers
as the evening drifts toward midnight

slow dancing in the dark shadows
of Leonard Cohen's dirge

feathery snow mounding on the graveyard gate
on the church bells on the outstretched hands

of the crescent moon rocking ever so slowly
in the graceful galactic rhythm of the fire's song

snap and flare of all things loosened and lost
winter moans in the stone cold bones

rock me now and turn me round
kiss me with your summer lips

waltz the winds of autumn till the bright colors
fall like stars and promises

pull me close to the drum of your heart
and call me by that name that answers the green

song of your need cries out in your dreams
call me by that name you learned

from the river's rush and the storm's bright lightning
say it now before I burn to ashes

and all we have is memory
lead me now by that name up the stairs

to the warm bed by the winter window
where we watch the words waltz white lace

through the dark sky falling as we are falling
through the long merciful silence

sing my name with your body burn it into my flesh
your lips brand the sweet wound of belonging.

II.

What They Didn't Say

It was in early summer when the green
lush grass pulses with juice
a thousand things to do freed from school

skipping down the sidewalk marbles in my pockets
waving a butterfly net
some second grade song looping

through the sun-drenched morning.
It was in early afternoon in the most quiet
time of day when not a single leaf stirs

when they took me to the garage
up the pull down stairs
to the small dirty attic
where the air was hot
and full of cobwebs.

Pretending I was a prisoner
they told me I had to take off all my clothes
as they sat with their sticks
and their serious faces watching.

I had no choice with their sticks
which they used to examine me.
I remember the rough wood floor
against my knees
against my stomach
against my back.
I don't remember breathing.

They didn't say my name had changed
but I knew.

The Difference

There is a way you want
a mouth to be hungry
for kisses
and the ripe tongue
and a way that a mouth
can devour you
the difference between
singing and the ripping that happens
somewhere between the throat and the gut.
There is a way you want
hands to be tender playful even searching
and a way hands can take and shame
make dark secrets in the dark
and wounds that fester in the flesh.
After all these years I still prefer
to make love in the light
where I can see everything.

Stolen

I would like to say
the body cannot be stolen.
I would like my heart to know
the body cannot be stolen.
But I have watched my body taken from me
watched from a high bridge of silence
above the heart pounding river
with its dark thrashing rapids.
I have watched my body say yes
when I was screaming no.
I have heard the sweet song from my body
choked out.
Yes the body can be stolen
and getting it back.

Glances Off

The blow
glances off
like the flint spark
how the body is steel
is shield
yet still taken
tied up with ropes
to the clothes tree
how they one by one
ice cubes
how the small rivers run
down the chest
down the belly
down the thighs
how they trace the rivers
with their laughter
how the rope burns
how my eyes close
how the rivers and
the shame

Scar Tissue

Proud flesh protects the wound
builds a healing circle
still the scar is witness.
And where the light has gone out
where the wound goes deep
where a song has been silenced how does the scar
build its shield in the body and the mind?
Touch me without knowing everything.
When I flinch or turn away it is not your fault
or my fault because the flesh
feels the knife long after the blood runs.
The body has learned the zoom out move
and the mind wanders far far away
when that forest of memories is set on fire
by the turn of a phrase or the turn of a touch
and I am trying to breathe in the heat
in the crackling air.

Dark Well

It is unsayable
because he says I can't tell
and because if I don't say it
maybe it didn't happen

I can't say it
even to myself
so how could I say it
out loud

and yet it plays
over and over
in the lonely mirror
and the night's dark dreams

plays again and again
in the scent of sweat
in the cold metal collision
of skin against skin

so now when
you take my hand like that
without thinking
I pull away

and the acid grief rises
from the deep well
where once words
clear as water.

A Way of Running

slap kiss strip
the name of their game
I am shivering nowhere to run
the walls of the garage shovel rake hoe hanging in perfect order
scent of old tires and grease
clay pots for growing
pretty flowers

how the mind
can follow the silk stream
of yellow light through the single small window
a way of running
away

slanting ray
bright like some saint's halo
until they throw my clothes outside on the green grass
to make me run naked
into the visible air

Who Never Pressed Charges

For all of us who never
pressed charges
never told the secret
never tried to explain
the paradox of flight and frozen limbs
how the throat tightens
and the fear rises like acid
when you try to speak

the days afterword
how the secret is raw
as you carry it through the day
sometimes right next to him
so you can hardly talk at all
but then you know you have to talk
as if nothing happened
so no one would ask questions
or think something was wrong

III.

Where Is the Soul?

Enter the sanctuary of grief.
Bring your memories, sorrows, questions.
The distance between then and now is closing,
the great welcome back home to earth,
to the breeze on skin, to raspberries.

If you open your hand to the day's offering
where the waves make their prayers,
lay their gifts on the altar,
pines stand straight as candles,
incense of pitch mingles with fog.

Tell me how many days will it take
to make your crossing
from doubt to forgiveness,
from the small boxes of speech to silence,
from love to hunger.

Where is the soul? Where are you looking?
How will you know when you find it?
Some bright vesicle in the vestibule of chance,
some unquenchable light
in the palm of the heart broken open.

At Mevlevi Monastery

The disciples of Rumi dance
on the last Sunday of the month. I expect
a performance but hope for a prayer,
for some shadow of the poet's passion
or the blade edge of a Sufi story. When the music starts
the wooden flute sings the hinges off my heart,
the cantor's voice is a river bending and falling,
surrendering to the sea. The dervishes enter
with measured steps, bow to each other
the deep bow of submission and drop
their black mantels of death.
With arms crossed on their chests they begin to turn,
slowly their white robes open like flowers. In one
fluid motion their arms loosen and rise,
their hands lift the whole world's petitions
in the whirling dance. Each swirling body
a prayer at the axis of the world
spinning gently into ecstasy, flowing
in the perfect circle of remembering everything
and forgetting everything. Whirling
the whole world awake, awake into silence,
each face now a doorway to heaven.
I stand and my whole body aches to dance
until all the questions melt away, until the center point
becomes every moment, every step, every word,
and the dance becomes my name, my home, my blood,
my blood, my home, my name.

Like a Mystic

I'm going to start living like a mystic
every morsel from the kitchen a sacrament
every bird song a dance toward Mecca

every space between words a cave of silence
where dawn shakes me by the shoulders and
I wake into that bright clearing of another breath

where nothing can be named where everything
disappears from the magician's hand
and the wind carries angels and doubt and all

the deeds of the ancestors murders and mercies
blow through the cells of my body like messengers
from Yahweh, Jesu, Allah, Krishna and the blood

on the lintel spells all the names of my slavery

Like a Poet

Then I will start living like a poet
on my knees pour the wild wine
down the throat of heaven
listen to the moon's full Om
and the geese flying their silver miles
mapless and certain in their elegant cacophony
I will not ask for reasons I will not pay the bills
but count the rust and butter petals of the Gloriosa
the sunflower's fringe of fire
until my heart tumbles into the long story
of clay and lightning
cell stamen bright bright wings
race of orbit bond of blood
how all the tender wounds weep
with the wine of compassion
and the bones in the crematorium
explode like stars
welcome the dark angel on the road east
I will erase the word tomorrow
and yesterday from the lexicon of time

Morning Glory

The morning glories climb
forever, spiral around anything
that will stand still and listen

to their lusty trumpets blare
the essence of amethyst and azure.
Where their flesh touches

trellis or branch, supple cells
rush to twirl, coil, circle,
like the gathering of elders

and children around the campfire,
always creating the round circuit
of faces facing each other, telling

their stories and knowing how
to hang on and reach upward.
Oh, to have such simple wisdom,

to have it live in your body,
to have such green flesh
that everywhere it touches

creates a circle, spiral of hope,
so the lush feast of the flower
can give itself away for the only

day it will ever have. Take
the next step without knowing
everything, without certainty

on the steep climb feeling for footholds.
Look for the circle, listen to the dream
calling in your marrow muscle blood.

Spiral toward hope, truth, bread,
like the morning glories with their wise
green hands climbing toward the light.

Sophia

I come from the silent desert
and the singing river,
from the dry desperation of failure and betrayal,
from the ecstasy of connection.

I know the alchemy
of metamorphosis and macrophage,
the seed, the seasons, the heart.

I call to you now from every doorway,
from the precipice of every hope.

Step into the river where everything
is flowing, brave the undercurrent
sucking at your ankles and scoop
the silver syllables to your face.

Drink it in, open your body, remember
the common code swimming
inside the helix of your marrow muscle blood.

And the light that leaps from you then
could be a word, a covenant, a bridge to peace.

Music Enters

The music enters like a hot sliver
under the skin,
sears the flesh with its rhythm,
troubles the waters that could heal you.
Let it climb the ladder of your spine.
One note like a tongue or a knife
opens you, one chord like the wind
through aspens shakes you awake.
One song like a wild fire licks at your feet
until you dance, dance out of your body,
dance out of your aloneness,
dance the rhythms of the rain,
of the river's wash
and the wing's whispered song
across the frantic sky.

Ancient Grains

I am making bread with ancient grains
emmer rice spelt tef
the old grains of Africa and Asia
primal hunger of heart and hearth
songs of earth and ocean
flour water and the deep well of dreams
how the yeast burrows and builds
honeycombs the dough
breathes in the warm pockets
of stillness
creates the architecture of body
crust and tenderness
tang and sweet.

I am making bread with my daughter
stories tears silence
the old grains of flesh and hope
primal hunger of heart and hearth
songs of earth and ocean
child grown child of her own
moon rising in her blood
how the years teach and test us
open into small pockets
of time honeycomb sweet
where we breathe in stillness
create the architecture of home
crust and tenderness
word and silence.

I am making bread with ancient grains
with my daughter
seed word time
primal hunger of heart and hearth
shaping the dough round
knead fold rise
in the soft stillness together
sliding our dreams and stories
onto the hot hearth stone
create the architecture of bread
crust and tenderness
hunger and home.

On the Path

I find on the path today
a soft gray nest of goose down,
with every step another small pinecone,
abundance of hope flung with wild abandon.
And leaves the color of pumpkins and fire,
finch feathers and wet clay, scarlet, sunset, siren.
Acorns and the perfect caps that acorns wear.
I find on the path today
a memory of bread,
the gift of her weekly ritual on Saturday morning,
pungent smell of yeast,
her hands always moving,
measure pour mix flour water salt.
And then the waiting
next to the window where the sun streamed in.
On the path today, how she would kneel and slide the six loaves
perfectly into the small oven in the corner of the small kitchen.
Our mouths would water with the smell of it baking.
On the path today, that warm bread
that always gathered us in a circle of enough.
Bread for the journey,
all we need,
bread that feeds me decades later
on the path today.

Winged

From where in the body
does the wing spring diaphanous
and bone

enough to bear the weight
of reason and death?
How does the body shape

the shape of hope
that lifts and glides
rises on the land's last breath?

Is the wing a vestige
of ventricle
when the heart

had not yet shut itself
behind the cage of bone?
Or a hinged vowel

from the story
in the voice
that levitates and sings?

Is wing crystallized need
from brain
or belly

the shape of longing

memorized in feathered flesh?
Tell me dear angel

with all your hovering madness
sleep with me tonight
above the reach of sight

and take me home
if only
for what may seem

a dream.

Dance at Dawn

Go out as far as you can
to sit alone on a stone throne
where you give up all the straight lines of your mind
in the dark quiet shiver an hour before dawn.
Set your eyes on that seam where water and sky
are stitched together in their great meeting
and when the fierce light tears the world wide
open for another day
dare to say your name
over the buckle and swell of waves
one sweet word of imperfect love
dare to say your name
not proud but in full voice
unfastened from any small hopes or pains.
Send it free as a smooth stone
skipping on the hammered blue
its singular dance
glancing gold in the new light
for a bright brief breath.

IV.

Grass

"I believe a leaf of grass is no less than the journeywork of the stars."
                                    —Walt Whitman

The precision of journeywork, exact
proportion and fit, matching the grain,
sanding to softness lacquered layers

of shine. Now make it all moving,
rowing its green body through the wind
or just glancing back and forth,

sun streaked electricity of glisten.
Make it changing and immutable,
essence and a million million faces

precise particular infinite. To bear
the crush of things, softening footsteps,
and the long months of ice. Who would

dare to rise again to celebrate
the circle of desire and fire? How
do you learn to bow like that, humble

bold elegant and with such large
measures of mercy and wrath?
White heat of the root probes for water

and holds tight, claws through clay,
branches like a river listening
to the pour of life. Architectures

of fiber and sway, arch pillar
wing, the palaces and palisades
of chloroplast and song. How the dew lays

its jewels along the arching
spine in the morning breeze, dawn's
fire reflected, the sigh of the grass.

Two Blue Herons

glide toward the shore
where I stand
watching the stars glitter
in the dark lake
and a seam
rips
some sharp synapse
fire to stone.

But not exactly that
of course.

Aren't we all
simply
collected sensory input
with cultural accretions

our eyes seeing
what we have words for
our ears able to hear
only part of the choir that sings and sings
from dawn to dawn?

What is the language of these
two blue monks
who gather their shawls
around their bodies
and stand strictly still
in the pellucid silence?

Will they give us
the syllables to name it?

Song of the Salmon

How many worlds ripen
in the nest of time,
how many universes are cracking
open, the small beaks of quasars
pecking inside the moment?

Every noun is foolishness
as if this light that lifts
in the east could be counted
photon by photon in its pilgrimage
through the galaxies.

Listen to the song of the salmon
returning to the stream of its birth
after months in the gravity of salt,
climbing the fresh currents,
thrashing its body against the gravel
to make the redd deep and safe
where its eggs will burst
like sleek silver syllables of hope.

Jays

Migration of blue bandits
brings the circus to my
wind-waltzing cedars
twenty then forty wheeling into trees
about the house
sapphire cobalt shine and bluster.
Tightrope walkers saunter along the branches.
Chattering clowns fill the yard with gossip.
I sit on the deck in the brisk air
heavy sweater and hot coffee
not to miss these bright mornings
edged with frost and farewell
these bold messengers that dare
to compare their plumage
with the falling gold and crimson.

Part of me in Venice at the market
listening to the haggling
over arugula and pears
the push and pull of banter
how each voice is a name
a particular cadence
how they all
become music and litany
cantor chorus alleluia and lament.

Less than an hour
and they take the show
to the next town.

I wonder what I missed
yesterday when I hit the snooze
button twice. Why sleep
when you can be
this awake
with lapis and azure wings?

Creation

The birds of creation weave strands of music
finch crow sparrow and dove
fly with wingspans of light years
beaks like sun flares
beating out of the east
weaving fine filaments of longing
with the silk of silence
for eons and ages
wheel from one end of heaven to the other
trailing their ribbons of fire and desire
until dawn licks the sky awake
light of the first morning
explosion of day
and then the long stories of stars
squint flame sputter
from birth to their final fierce sparks
lapse into dark
song-shaped hole in the sky.
And floating among the stars
a luminescent nest of possibility
chrysolite jasper granite and schist
rock and water lightning and longing.
And in a million million years
the tiny seeds of hope crack the code of green
flame out in balsam elm palm
beech birch oak
and every caterwauling color of blossom flower fruit
plum apple fig
dandelion daisy morning glory glory.

And with a zillion million combinations
marvel of animal
amoeba sponge eel dolphin
and the frenzy onto land when fins turn to feet
and those who stand upright begin to wonder
brains imagine.
Then music and words
that tell the story of the birds
of creation weaving the strands
of fire and desire.

Language Acquisition

They wanted to know how a word is learned,
how the saying of the word happens
out of the cacophony of vocables, syllables,
sentences, songs, arguments and the long stories
when it seems no one is listening; so they brought
their baby home to a house full of cameras
that watched and listened for sounds, how words
might emerge from the rivers of lexemes.

Now they have a billion bits of data about how
to learn a word, how to say a word, how it comes
from the mapped intersections of laughter, love
and explanation, patterns in the social environment.
They can play the video so you can hear their son
learn the word for water, cascading from gibberish
to the word itself: gaga, gawa, gatcwha, wata, water
in six months. They can play every trace of language
he heard and how the adults would subconsciously
restructure their talk to make it simple and clear.
They speak of continuous capture and feedback loops.

I wonder how the word settles in some small hollow
of his heart, how water connects with the softness of night
and the sweet music of the rain, his mother's hands,
the smell of the blue blanket, and how later he will say it
slowly to settle himself before he speaks, when all the cameras
are watching and he must try to say exactly what he means.

In the Silence

footsteps crunch on the cold snow
heaven's full of falling mercy
the big arms of the pine
spread in prayer shawled in white
the whole everyday machine muffled

if everyone could say their name
in such silence we might hear
each one might send their small swirl
of hopes and prayers
spiraling out like sufi robes
in the dervish dance
and we might all
hear each other's hands rise up
and we would know the one world's song

all our rituals are attempts at listening
all our songs a preparation
for emptiness when our words
have all fallen away because we know
we are all whirling together

wherever you are however you do it
notice how we are all whirling together
in the great round dance
on this tiny rock with fire in its soul
through the grand galaxies
spinning with mercy and wonder

Jacob's Ladder

When you are on the ladder with a paint brush
twenty feet of air between you and the ground
do not swing in anger or fear at the yellow jackets.

If angels are ascending and descending the ladder
of your spine let them stretch their strands of light
into the small spaces between the discs of bone.

When you notice the way your heart can lean
toward shadow pay attention to the story
you keep telling yourself as if it were the truth.

If you are keeping track of the times you
fold the laundry or take out the garbage
you are not an angel ascending or descending.

When you curse the baby bunny eating lettuce
from the garden it is time to notice and listen
how the angels sing of mercy and bread.

If the spider is crawling up your sleeve
use your opposable thumb and consider the vow
of the bodhisattva and the levels of humility.

When you forget to roll up the car window
before the rain storm think of each silver drop
as an angel descending with blessed reminders.

Human Robotics Project

The reality recognition and sensory software engineers
realized, after a day of silence during the retreat at which
the shaman required they sit in silence together
for twenty-four hours watching their minds work
and noticing the insistent conversations
in the veins muscles cells of their bodies, that none
of the sensory inputs could be pre-loaded, a communal
insight that rippled through the field of their creative
consciousness formed by their close working together
on the human robotics project that each of them had longed for,
the final test of their talents, they realized that none of the sensory
inputs could be pre-loaded, that only the process for engaging
with the world and connecting the sensory inputs with each other
and with the joy state, the name they had agreed upon
for the spectrum of positive to negative dispositions of the unit,
could be made part of the base operating system, but that each
sensory input must happen in the full context of the experience
itself so the smell of bread baking would not only signal
bread in the reality recognition mother board but everything
else that might be associated with hunger, home, butter,
the way she hugged you when you got home from school,
the small whistle of the tea kettle and the story she told
over and over about her teacher giving her the old violin
that she had learned to play as if it had its own voice and all
she needed to do was coax it carefully out of silence,
so when the unit at some time in the future would smell
bread baking, all of this and more would come flooding
back into the mother board and the past reality itself would
somehow expand into the present and flow into the future
so the joy state registers the possibility of the self existing.

Greenest Grass

The greenest grass is divided and chalked,
measured for boundaries and goals.
It calls to the young shirtless men
aching for points, for records, for the contest
that proves. It feels the lightning feet,
the wild jumps, hears the cheers and applause
but still it calls to the quick muscled boys.

Come to me, come to me in moonlight,
in silence lay your back in this soft
cradle. Trophies rust and bleachers
empty but always the stars speak
your names on the clear nights of summer.

Chopping Birch

In half a heartbeat, before the axe head
drops, I see the Morse code in the birch bark,
clear signs of language, the lettered story circling
into speech, how the merciless wind on the high

ledge brought this tall soldier down. But first
how it swayed, how the rim shot riffs of its white
fingers cracked and clattered through the storm,
how it swung in a painful arc through the sky

like God's metronome keeping time to the song
of everything that dies too soon too soon too soon
and how its roots snapped and shattered like bone,
how it fell battering its brothers and sisters,

sheering off their close branches, scarring their trunks
as its hands clawed at the whistling air. The axe head
drops, white flesh parts, clean separation into pieces
to fit the fireplace. Later I listen to its sad lament,

the song now leaping from its red lips, a final plea
to hear its story before all that's left is ashes.

Directions

All morning the rain falls in whispers
soft drops and mists of mercy.
The wet bells of the purple columbine
toll their purple notes.
Slick grass recites the essence of green.
The river is calling your name
reaching for you with its long arms.
If you stay where you are content
with being lost you might turn
toward the silence with longing.

You've been a stranger to yourself
for too long now stop looking in the mirror.
You don't have to figure it out.
Pretend the whole sky is your home
but you can't put the stars in your pockets.
The moon has its own reasons.

You don't have to figure it out.
The grass will outlive us for sure
without the opposable thumb.
This is no reason for hopelessness
no reason to give up you must go on
trying without effort or expectation.
Even when the fish are dying
you must give the children their names.

The children will not ask for directions.
As they always have they will think

they are invincible until they are lost
in the rain in the morning in the purple
river of memory. But if you love them
they will learn to seek the silence
they will learn to let the rain wash over
them in waves and waves of mercy.

First Question

Tell me how
how did it begin
that first question
some small space between instinct and act

brief doubt
glitch in the chemistry of synapse
beyond the lizard brain
did the soul happen then

in that tiny space of wonder
like some cosmic chrysalis
lure of hope
push of pure light

toward the next threshold of longing
did the heart open
its chamber of compassion
did the eye recognize itself

in the mirror of the other's face.

First Song

The first song he learned in school held the pieces
to all the words in the world. As she tapped their lithe
bodies posted above the blackboard with her long pointer

he sang each one and catalogued the world by their names.
A is for apple, antler, aardvark. B is for boy, bat, baseball.
C is for cat, comb, cougar. D is for dog, door, daughter.

The whole world went like this. You could hitch them
together like cars on a train and they took in the big
universe one word at a time, nothing was left out.

At night in his room, he made lists from the dictionary.
He started with three words for each letter, then five,
ten, thirty, a hundred. Whenever he heard a new word

he put it in its proper column, it belonged to A or D or K.
Later there were states and their capitals,
all the bones, muscles and systems of the body;

but they all fit in one of the columns absolutely
and for sure. The lists were very long now,
some words hyphenated or with five sibilant syllables.

In history class, he learned the names of wars. Starting
with his own country and the revolution: A is for Augusta,
B is for Bunker Hill and Brandywine, C is for Concord,

Charleston, Camden; then marching through the years
of the Civil War: A is for Antietam, B is for Bull Run,
C is for Chattanooga, D is for Donelson,

F is for Fredericksburg, G is for Gettysburg,
H is for Harper's Ferry; column by never ending column,
on to the World Wars: One: Antwerp, Belleau Wood,

Caporetto, Delville Wood, Es Sinn, Falluja, Gorizia,
Hill 60, Isonzo, Jutland, Krithia, Lone Pine, Mughar Ridge,
Namur, Passchendaele, Ramadi, Scarborough, Tannenberg,

Verdun, Wadi, Ypres, and WWII: Attu, Aleutian Islands,
Battle of the Bulge, Bismarck Sea, Christmas Island,
Crucifix Hill, Denmark Strait, Dragoon, El Alamein,

Operation Elephant, Fontenay, Guadalcanal, Halbe,
Iwo Jima, Imphal, Java, Java Sea, Kwajalein, Kiev,
Luzon, Litani River, Midway, Madagascar, Mindinao,

North Borneo, Netherlands, Odessa, Peleliu, Pearl Harbor,
Operation Queen, Rennell Island, Somaliland, Smolensk,
Saipan, Tinian, Taranto Harbor, Operation Torch,

Visayas, Operation Varsity, Wake Island, Warsaw Uprising.
Then, on to ancient lands and smaller countries, on every
continent, in every year, lines drawn and redrawn and redrawn,

small hills taken and lost on the same day, cities renamed, maps
reconfigured, blood from the beaches painting the lips of the waves,
the children's song all grown up, fed by history

and the weeping stars and the weeping mothers.
As he filled notebooks with columns of wars and the names of each
fallen soldier in every uniform, and an X for each civilian

casualty: children, mothers, fathers, grandfathers and grandmothers,
he began to ask a question: where is the small gland that screams
for victory and land, the aberrant cyst in the anterior cingulated gyrus,

the trigger glyph in the right-handed double helix that keeps repeating
itself like the simplest song: ABCDEFGHIJKLMNOPQRSTUVWXYZ
Now I know my ABCs, next time won't you sing with me.

Homeland Poetry

when I become head of homeland poetry
or director of the department of natural poetics
or czar of the world bank of words

I will create an army a loosely confederated
slightly crazy army of lyrical liars
trying to tell the truth

who march out of step
question every command
give out poems and lunch vouchers at the bus stops

wander the streets listening
how the tenderness of the heart tells its story
we will lurk in the shadows

made by the full moon
we will have uniforms
of every color and cut

yellow silk red satin cobalt corduroy
tutus and togas
short shorts and bell bottoms

some will be tunics tailored for star catching
or tight jackets of rhyme and meter
or long duster coats of leather and thirst

all embroidered with the shapes of birds

and smeared with the blood of the lost and the found
we will have weapons

wonder sharpened to the edge of dawn
improvised explosive laughter
questions strapped to our bodies

megatons of ammo metaphor
to rearrange reality
and demolish the temples of scarcity

mushroom clouds of prayers rising
carrying the cries
of betrayal and the incantations of light

we will learn the martial arts
dancing in the alleys of forgetfulness
and drumming on the dumpsters of need

standing in one place
in the postures of wonder
listening to the children sing with their whole bodies

we will unbuckle uncover unshackle
until the whispers on the fire escape
are amplified in the cathedrals

until the shattered dreams of the never heard
and the silent wishes of the children
are written in the laws of the land

we will hear the songs
of the children who even in their sleep
sing with their whole bodies

sing with their lips and bones and open hands
hold me hold me hold me now and the whole world around me
hold my body my river my wonder my wild

we will be the army of the lost and found
singing the songs of the children
in courthouses and senate chambers

singing their hunger and their hope
singing for their rivers and green valleys
singing for their bread

V.

What Are You Seeking

What are you seeking
to be of use a voice that matters
to be the wild
essence
of your individual question
the one that wakes you in the night
visits in the gut of your knowing

Listen then
bend to the earth
your ear to the voices of the children
to the suffering that runs
like untamed horses
stampede of need
for water rice hope

Count the calluses on the hands
of the children chained to the work table
the empty eyes
bellies aching for bread
measure the continents
as they drift farther apart
the galaxies
spinning deeper
into space

Why are you waiting
grab on anywhere
find your own embrace and hold
on tight
kiss
the wounds

Witness

The lead man with his dented
lunch pail and the caged bird
starts down the mine shaft
a few steps ahead of the others
and if the bird stops singing
he watches it very carefully
and if it drops from the perch
like a stone he turns yells runs.

Decades later with wise
instruments we measure the toxins
in the air and the water the barrels
of spillage the micrograms
of poison. But how many feathered
messengers will it take how many
creatures must give witness?

Winnowing

Spines stiff with harvest
hands full of stories
babies bundled in wishes on their backs
they lift the brimming baskets
high into the breeze
and let the beans fall
like water or laughter
and the wind winnows
their hopes and sorrows
takes the chaff and leaves
almost enough for all
the hungry bellies

With each new basket
a new song old
as this verdant valley
a song that links them together
like prisoners
or family
under this hot stare
in this hot valley
where life was born
steaming and singing

And the babies
how the rhythms enter
their marrow
blood borne longing
sweet desire

songs stitched into the small
pockets of their cells
if they are lucky
there will be enough beans
and the songs will find
their voices
in the hungry valley
where the wind winnows
every skin

Red Line

As the sun breaks this winter morning
and sends a filament of pulsing scarlet
across the horizon as if a scalpel cut
one thin incision and life seeped
then poured out bleeding the day
at that moment when the blade touches
and the red line runs
a picture comes
at this edge of dawn knowing.

A red detonation cord that you are
connecting with your thin fingers
running through the lining of the black
leather suicide vest. The wire catches
on your right breast where you hoped
your baby's perfect lips would suck.

Are you thinking of some verse from the Koran
as you rub your bulging belly or are you still
feeling the soft signature of your lover's last kiss?
Are you wondering where the ball bearings
will lodge in the bodies of your enemy?
Are you wondering how your flesh with separate and scatter?

What is your name? And last night
could you sleep? Did you sing a familiar
lullaby to the promise taking shape
just under your heart waiting in the dark
ocean of your womb for the red line of dawn?

Meeting of the Higher Powers

Only the higher powers were called
to the meeting with its one question
how can we open their eyes
not because of the improvised explosive devices
not because of the high walls on the borders
or immigrants and refugees wandering
the deserts and the hungry streets
not because of the white egret's wings
oiled black and the rank rivers running
with poison in the veins of the poor
not because of all the names for god
or the rites and rules to keep the others out.

She was standing straight as a lightning bolt
her cheek bones brushed with dawn
and in her arms a child without breath
taut skin over the ribs and swollen belly
she kissed with such tenderness the small lifeless body.

Could the human brain in its next evolution
escape its protective fear its solitary illusion
could the hands grow large again
might these human kind hear the common heart drum
in the common precious flesh
could they learn again the art of bread?

Inimba

Seven mothers and their families mourning the deaths
of their seven sons meet with the young man, perpetrator,
police informant, who turned his back on his people for profit,
for safety, for shame. Only the mothers speak when he asks
for their forgiveness. They tell him he sold his own blood
to the white apartheid government. He was a wolf.
He shakes as he listens, his face twitching, and pleads
haltingly, softly, addressing the mothers, "My parents
I ask your forgiveness from the bottom of my heart."
It is not his words that move her. There is a long silence
after his plea. The whole story wells up without sound,
how limitless the losses, how unsayable the sins, and yet

she says, "You are the same age as my murdered son,
Christopher. I want to tell you, my son, that I,
as Christopher's mother, I forgive you, my son."
She says "my son" and embraces him, presses his body
to her body, a child, her wayward child, a child forgiven.
Later, when they ask her how she could forgive him,
she speaks of her womb, of the umbilical cord
that joins a mother to a child, of that feeling for a child,
how a mother knows her child's desperation or longing
for home when he is in trouble even a thousand miles away.
She speaks of the feeling in her body, she calls it
"inimba," umbilical tether, the cord that binds us all.

In Circles

We place ourselves in circles and huddles,
knowing somehow that this way of being together
signs the shape of our dreams and longings.

From space we see ourselves round,
connected to one another, facing each other,
with all our differences dancing around the sun together.

For centuries we have been trying to bring
the circle down from mystery skies,
to set it stone solid in our hearts, to memorize
the knowing of each preciousness
equally gift to the circle of whole.

Spirals etched in red rock canyon story the journey
out of and into the center that holds all things together.
Stonehenge pillars and lintels dragged for miles,
scraped into meaning, set in sacred formation with sun and moon.
Conical mounds heaped into remembrance
ritual the lives of elders who circle the fire of the tribe.
Everywhere and ancient the circle
is repeated, shaping us to its original wisdom.

Give us each day our daily hunger,
to be more than we are now,
to be less solitary selves doubting our place,
to be more a circle of connection and acceptance,
spherical harmony of the heavens.
Each one a single voice, a sacred story,
but always in the larger circle of meaning and mystery.

Immigrants

To Piedra Herrada and Rosario
and the other high sanctuaries
the monarchs come from the north
vagrants drifters unstopped
by walls or laws or border guards
or the helicopter patrol over the desert
pulled by longing and the slant of light
by the large un-nameable orbits
ride the waves risk the strong winds
for months and generations mass themselves
on the great trees layers upon layers
of filament wings pulsing in the sun
six or seven deep bodies clinging to bodies
so that when the frost comes in January
the inside layers will be protected
and the martyrs will drop like leaves
to the forest floor as the moon's silver
arms hold us all in the dark shivering
with our small questions counting
the hungry hands the broken wings
in the Pima County morgue in Tucson
where the body bags are stacked on stainless
steel shelves from floor to ceiling
Hector
Roberto
Miguel
40 bodies
in two weeks in July when the night
temperatures were at record highs

still they come from the mountain villages
and the breadless streets in the city
for a chance to send some hope back home
where the monarchs come year after year
crossing the limits of our small geographies
on the buoyant wings of hunger

Holy Night

Holy is not the cross of suffering,
not the long night of grief, holy is birth, bread, every act
or word that longs for dawn, leans toward the light.

In stables, caves, cathedrals we whisper
our prayers, sing in the dialects of constellations. Still the galaxies
drift apart, universe shatters into hatred and tears. Another bomb

blast in the market, a young girl stands
with her bloody hands lifted to the sky. At her feet the body
of her sister, the one who always protected her, held her hand

on the way to school, read her stories in the dark
unholy nights rumbling with guns. What will take us from this
long legacy of fear to a new belonging, from this ritual of destruction

with all its ammo and assumptions? How shall we build
bridges across such chasms, centuries wide and deep as the shape
and color of our bodies and our names? Do you hear the grandfather

calling over the clouds of dust and the din of sirens,
calling her name and her sister's name? She answers only
with her hands held up to the sky, her whole body wants to be invisible,

to be yesterday, to be anything but now. How shall we
make a world out of this much sadness with our feeble desire
for peace? Shall we make a pilgrimage to this pieta? Shall we search

the heavens for a star? Love is not a river or a lily
but something cobbled together by day and night, a fragile
dwelling built out of found objects: stories, tears, hope.

Grasshopper

On my walk along the slow brown river
I find one grasshopper with its golden
belly split and splayed on a stone

altar like some small ritual accompanied
by daisies and their fringes of fire.
I watch hundreds of dusty grasshoppers

fling the brown crusts
of their bodies out of the dry grass,
how the machinery

of their wings and the springs
in their legs fold tight and then explode.
It seems like perfection, precision,

until I notice how they almost never
land on their feet, how they struggle to right
themselves after every frantic flight. I see

then the dizzy dance of hunger,
burnished bullet of gut seeking anything
green. Back in my hotel room on the TV

the children in Haiti are barricaded
behind razor wire to keep them
from rioting as the rice is unloaded,

their wracked bodies

like x-rays, a boy licks his lips when the grains
pour from a ripped burlap bag.

Some of the children are tangled in the wire,
bleeding, pushed by others so overcome
with want, they could not stop running

toward the trucks full of food.
Why not the feast with the whole table
full, why not the bread broken

and wine poured out more than enough?
Who writes the story to include this grasshopper
split open, these brown bellies bloated,

this muddy river that runs through Kearney,
these daisies shaking with light,
a story that doesn't leave

anything out, not one single scream?

Enhanced Interrogation

He had been chosen
for the special assignment
the special training
in enhanced interrogation.
Anything to protect his family
his country he thought.
Now the worst of it
happened at night
when his 3 year old son
would call from his bedroom
Daddy Daddy I'm thirsty.
In the darkness
in the silence
when he ran the water
into the glass
that sound would bounce
off the bathroom walls
and echo in his skull
as if he were pouring the water
over the face of his captive
covered with the cloth
and pouring the water over
that mouth and nose
he would panic like the prisoner .
his throat would tighten
and the pounding would begin
again in his lungs and heart.
Then he would sit
on the edge of his son's bed

trying not to tremble
and tell him everything
would be alright
dragons are make believe
they can't get inside you
and the darkness is for sleeping
dreaming good dreams.

Colombia Displaced

And then I saw a man
take out a gun
and shoot my father
she says
without tears
her huge brown eyes boring
into each person
her black hair
pulled back tight.

She is older
than her 13 years
strong for her crying mother
whose words she translates
into perfect English
for the audience.

I have come to hear
the statistics the politics.
But here is the body of her father
collapsed at the door
which she says he always answered
because there were so many
who came for bread
for words to hang onto
when their land was taken
their jobs lost
their homes burned.

The blood
unstoppable
as her mother screams
and she and her brothers run for help
too late.

What she does not say:
How to sleep in that house.
How to step over the stain
at the door
going and coming back.
How to listen for unfamiliar voices.
How to sleep in the dark.
How to sleep through the dreams.
How to sleep.

Banquet

I am trying to gather them all
for the banquet
all the children
running barefoot
toward the dirt floor school
where each one should have a yellow pencil
and a thick piece of bread.
I am trying to comfort the sick children
with their curious eyes
every wound the world howling.
I want to tell their mothers
there will be enough cornmeal
so they don't have to mix it with clay
to dull the hunger in the night.
I want to dig so deep
that the well will never give up
to fill each palm
with rice and beans
each belly with a word
each ragged pocket with a promise
they could count on.
I am running
in my sleep to gather
all the children
for the banquet
so little time before the awful howling
howling in the desert
no manna.

After Sandy Hook

I am following the directions
of the meditation to slowly peel the ordinary
orange breathe deep the spice sweet scent
and separate its perfect sections
when I notice how the body has so many ways
to fold and bend the human body with nearly
350 bones when it is just born which fuse
together on their own intricate timetable
into 206 grown up bones
14 facial bones for joy and grief
106 bones in the hands and feet
for doing what hands and feet do at the heart's bidding
still I exhaust myself with questions
when every step could be an infinite
journey into the land of mercy
where the newspapers do not argue about the number
of bullets our guns should hold
or how the children who go to school skipping and singing
can forget there are so many ways
the human body can fold and bend and fall
with all its perfect bones and its precious face.

Give Yourself

Give yourself to the path
to each step each word each moment
each small mercy each held hand
each meeting of the eyes.
Give yourself and the way will find you
and guide you.
You may do your planning
your careful calculations balance the checkbook
pay the bills park between the lines.
But when the time comes for dancing
listen to the wind
turn and turn as the music beckons
as the path lures you.
Sink to your knees in the center
of your calling your wounds and all
your wild longings.
Speak the question at the center
of your wisdom breathe in the betrayals and the chains.
Forgive yourself again.
Then stand in the center
all the bold tree of you
stand at the center of the world.
Be anointed be chosen again
for the only work
large enough for your heart
for your wonder and your wandering.
Be chosen again to live
in that fierce question
that sets your heart on fire.

Notes

Preparing the Soil: On Ash Wednesday, which begins the Christian season of Lent, ashes in the sign of the cross are applied to the penitent's forehead, often accompanied with the traditional reminder "Remember that you are dust and unto dust you shall return."

Mother's Story: Solanus Casey was an American Capuchin friar and priest who was known for working wonders and for his deep faith and humility. He served at St. Bonaventure Monastery in Detroit for 21 years.

At Mevlevi Monastery: The Galata Mevlevihanesi monastery in Istanbul was founded in 1491. Its first leader was Muhammed Semai Sultan Divani, a descendant of Mevlana Jelalledin Rumi who founded the Mevlevi Sufi order.

Language Acquisition: Based on the TED talk by Deb Roy "The Birth of a Word."

Jacob's Ladder: See Genesis chapter 28.

Winnowing: Based on the wood cut print by the same name by Uganda artist Fred Mutebi.

Inimba: Based on a story from the truth and reconciliation hearings in South Africa narrated by Pumla Gobodo-Madikizela in *Forgiveness and the Maternal Body: An African Ethics of Interconnectedness* (Ann Arbor: Fetzer Institute, 2011).

About the Author

GARY BOELHOWER's poetry has been published in anthologies: *Amethyst and Agate: Poems of Lake Superior*, Holy Cow! Press (2015), *The Heart of All That Is: Reflections on Home*, Holy Cow! Press (2013), *The Cancer Poetry Project 2*, Tasora Books (2013), *Beloved on the Earth: 150 Poems of Grief and Gratitude*, Holy Cow! Press (2009), *Trail Guide to the Northland Experience in Prints and Poetry*, Calyx Press Duluth (2008), and *County lines: 87 Minnesota Counties 130 Minnesota Poets*, Loonfeather Press (2008) and in journals and magazines: *America, Duluth Superior Symphony Orchestra Magazine, The Freshwater Review, Lake Superior Magazine, New Millenium Writings, Out of Words, Plainsongs, Prove, Shavings*, and *Willow Review*. His 2011 collection of poems, *Marrow, Muscle, Flight* (Wildwood River Press) won the Midwest Book Award. He was awarded the Foley Prize in poetry from *America* magazine in 2012 and a career development grant from the Arrowhead Regional Arts Council in 2010.

His recent nonfiction books include *Choose Wisely: Practical Insights from Spiritual Traditions*, Paulist Press (2013) and *Mountain 10: Climbing the Labyrinth Within*, (co-authored with Joe Miguez and Tricia Pearce) Mountain Ten Resources (2013). Boelhower teaches at The College of St. Scholastica in Duluth, Minn. in ethics, spirituality, and leadership. He has held leadership positions in higher education, including chair of humanities, dean of life-long learning, dean of graduate studies and vice president for academic affairs. He has created non-profit community organizations for feeding the hungry and for adult literacy. He has consulted with and provided training for a broad range of organizations on dialogue, authentic leadership, values and vision, the respectful workplace, and wise decision-making.

About the Cover Artist

KATE WHITTAKER recently moved from Duluth, MN to Shelburne Falls, MA, where she continues to make images that speak to her interests in patterns and rhythms found in nature, how the human species effects these patterns, from ancient times to present.

Her website is: *www.katewhittaker.com*